A1 - A2 ENGLISH

CONVERSATIONS IN EASY ENGLISH

Premium Languages

PRACTICE YOUR CONVERSATIONAL SKILLS IN REAL SITUATIONS

Premium Languages LTD

Layout: www.jgarridomaquetacion.com

The limits of my language are the limits of my world.
(Ludwig Wittgenstein)

TABLE OF CONTENTS

PERSONAL INFORMATION

▶ CONVERSATION 1

— **Official:** What's your name?
— **John:** My name is John.
— **Official:** What's your last name?
— **John:** My last name is Carter Smith.
— **Official:** What's your nationality?
— **John:** I'm American.
— **Official:** Where do you live?
— **John:** I live in Chicago.
— **Official:** What's your address?
— **John:** 45 Maple Street, Apartment 12.
— **Official:** How old are you?
— **John:** I'm 28 years old.
— **Official:** Are you married?
— **John:** No, I'm single.
— **Official:** Do you have any children?
— **John:** No, I don't.
— **Official:** What do you do for a living?
— **John:** I'm a software engineer.
— **Official:** What's your phone number?
— **John:** It's 555-123-4567.
— **Official:** What's your email address?
— **John:** It's john.carter.smith@pmail.com.

▶ CONVERSATION 2

- **Secretary:** What's your full name?
- **Candidate:** Emily Johnson Clark.
- **Secretary:** Where do you currently live?
- **Candidate:** In Los Angeles.
- **Secretary:** What's your complete date of birth?
- **Candidate:** March 15, 1988.
- **Secretary:** Place of birth?
- **Candidate:** San Diego, California.
- **Secretary:** Your address, please?
- **Candidate:** 1234 Sunset Boulevard.
- **Secretary:** Occupation?
- **Candidate:** Financial analyst.
- **Secretary:** And your marital status?
- **Candidate:** Married.
- **Secretary:** Do you have any children?
- **Candidate:** Yes, two. A boy and a girl.
- **Secretary:** What does your husband do for a living?
- **Candidate:** He's an insurance agent.
- **Secretary:** Do you have a landline?
- **Candidate:** No, just a mobile phone. It's 555-789-1234.
- **Secretary:** A contact email, please.
- **Candidate:** emily.j.clark@email.com.

1. Answer the following questions with your personal information.

- What is your full name?

- Where do you currently live?

- What is your full date of birth?

- Place of birth?

- Occupation?

- And your marital status?

- Do you have children?

- Phone number?

- A contact email, please.

---

2. Write questions for these answers.

- My name is Robert.

_____

- My surname is Smith.

_____

- Los Angeles, California.

_____

- I am 36 years old.

_____

- February 15th.

_____

- Independence Street, number 45.

_____

- Married.

_____

- Yes, one daughter.

_____

- I am a project manager at a bank.

_____

- Robert.Smith@mail.com

_____

- 290-78-90-32

_____

DAILY ROUTINE

▶ CONVERSATION 1

- **Paula:** What time do you wake up?
- **Lydia:** I wake up every day at 7 a.m.
- **Paula:** Do you have a morning routine?
- **Lydia:** Yes, I usually shower right after waking up. Then I get dressed and have breakfast in the kitchen.
- **Paula:** What do you usually have for breakfast?
- **Lydia:** I almost always have cereal with milk.
- **Paula:** And how do you get to work?
- **Lydia:** I take a bus and then walk for about 10 minutes to get to the office.
- **Paula:** How long does it take you to get from home to the office?
- **Lydia:** No more than 30 or 35 minutes.
- **Paula:** What time do you take your lunch break?
- **Lydia:** We take a break at 1 p.m. and go back to work at 2 p.m.
- **Paula:** What time do you finish work?
- **Lydia:** It depends on the week, but usually between 6 p.m. and 6:30 p.m.
- **Paula:** Do you do anything after work?
- **Lydia:** Yes, on Mondays and Wednesdays I go to the gym. On Tuesdays and Thursdays, I have Spanish classes.
- **Paula:** And on Fridays?
- **Lydia:** On Fridays, I go out for a beer with my friends.
- **Paula:** What time do you go to bed on workdays?
- **Lydia:** Always before midnight. I need at least 7 hours of sleep.

▶ CONVERSATION 2

- **John:** Do you wake up very early in the mornings?
- **Emily:** It depends. Sometimes I have to get up at 6 a.m., and other days at 8 a.m. Two or three days a week, I get up earlier to go for a run.
- **John:** Ugh, I can't wake up that early because I always go to bed very late. I watch TV until 2 a.m. or later.
- **Emily:** That's really late, isn't it?
- **John:** Yes, but I also wake up late and have a big breakfast with eggs and sausages. After that, I don't eat until the afternoon.
- **Emily:** I prefer to eat lightly in the morning and have lunch at 12 p.m.
- **John:** And do you have to take the subway to get to work?
- **Emily:** Yes, every day. It's always very crowded.
- **John:** I work from home, and it's very peaceful.
- **Emily:** Isn't it a bit boring?
- **John:** No, I only work 4 or 5 hours, and sometimes I go out for a walk.
- **Emily:** Do you work every day?
- **John:** I work in the afternoons from Monday to Friday.
- **Emily:** I have to work on Saturday mornings, so I go to bed early on Fridays.
- **John:** We have very different lives.
- **Emily:** Yes, I think so.

EXERCISES

1. Describe your daily routine using the reference from the previous dialogues:

_____

_____

_____

_____

_____

_____

_____

_____

_____

_____

_____

_____

_____

_____

_____

_____

_____

_____

_____

2. Think of a famous person you like and imagine what their daily routine is like:

_____

_____

_____

_____

_____

_____

_____

_____

_____

_____

_____

_____

_____

_____

_____

_____

_____

THE WEEKEND

— **Thomas:** Hi, Sam, what are you doing this weekend?

— **Sam:** Honestly, I have a lot to do this weekend. On Saturday, it's my sister Beatrice's birthday, and we're throwing a surprise party at my house. On Sunday morning, I want to play tennis with my friend, and then I'm going out to an Italian restaurant with my wife for lunch.

— **Thomas:** Wow, I see you're really busy.

— **Sam:** What about you? What are you doing?

— **Thomas:** On Saturday morning, I'm going to rest. I need to sleep because I've been really tired this week. In the afternoon, my dad wants to go to the stadium to watch the soccer match. On Sunday, I'm going for a run in the park, and then we'll probably go to a bar for some beers.

— **Sam:** Sometimes, I go running in the park too.

— **Thomas:** Why don't we go together next week?

— **Sam:** Yeah, that's a good idea.

— **Thomas:** We can run 10 kilometers and then grab a beer together.

— **Sam:** Perfect!

— **Thomas:** Is 12 p.m. okay?

— **Sam:** Better at 11 a.m. I have something to do at 2 p.m., and I need to be home a little earlier.

— **Thomas:** Sounds good. I'll call you next week to confirm.

EXERCISES

1. Answer the following questions:

- What time do you usually get up on Sundays?

- Do you have the same breakfast as during the week?

- Do you play sports on weekends?

- What are your plans for this weekend?

- Do you go to bed very late on weekends?

- Do you watch a lot of television during the weekends?

2. Describe what the perfect weekend is like for you:

THE HOUSE

▶ CONVERSATION 1

— **Rachel:** Do you still live in the same house as last year?

— **Philip:** No, we live in a new house now. It's really nice and much bigger than the old one.

— **Rachel:** That's great! What's it like?

— **Philip:** It's a modern house with 4 bedrooms, two bathrooms, a big kitchen, and a living room with a huge sofa.

— **Rachel:** Does it have a garden?

— **Philip:** Yes, it has a small garden with plants and a patio.

— **Rachel:** We're still in the same house, but we're doing some renovations. We want to expand the kitchen and change the living room furniture: the table, chairs, sofa, bookshelves…

▶ CONVERSATION 2

— **Oscar:** I need a central apartment, with lots of light and close to the subway station.

— **Agent:** How many bedrooms?

— **Oscar:** Just one or two bedrooms.

— **Agent:** Furnished or unfurnished?

— **Oscar:** Furnished is better. I don't want to have to buy beds, wardrobes, etc.

— **Agent:** Modern or traditional style?

— **Oscar:** It's not important, but I want good quality.

EXERCISES

1. Answer the following questions about your home:

- How many rooms does it have?

_____

- How many bathrooms does it have?

_____

- What is the kitchen like?

_____

- What do you like most about your house?

_____

- What's in your living room?

_____

- What part of your house would you like to change?

_____

2. Describe what your ideal home is like:

_____

_____

_____

_____

THE NEIGHBOURHOOD

▶ CONVERSATION 1

— **Mark:** My neighbourhood is the best.

— **Derek:** Why do you say that?

— **Mark:** Because in my neighbourhood, we have everything.

— **Derek:** Really?

— **Mark:** Yes, there's a huge park for exercising. There are two cinemas and lots of restaurants of all kinds.

— **Derek:** And shops?

— **Mark:** Yes, really good shops for food and clothes.

— **Derek:** And there's also a big library, right?

— **Mark:** Yes, but I never go to the library.

— **Derek:** Is it well-connected?

— **Mark:** It has a train station and lots of buses.

— **Derek:** Yes, but there's a lot of traffic in your neighbourhood.

— **Mark:** That's true, traffic is a problem.

— **Derek:** And it's a bit expensive too.

— **Mark:** It's actually very expensive.

— **Derek:** Also, it's far from the city center.

— **Mark:** It's about 40 minutes by bus.

— **Derek:** I think your neighbourhood doesn't have a school, does it?

— **Mark:** It has one, but it's very small.

— **Derek:** Well, but you really like it, and that's what matters.

▶ CONVERSATION 2

- **Anna:** I don't know which neighbourhood is better… I like both.
- **Laura:** Well, the Rosewood neighbourhood is more modern and closer to the city center.
- **Anna:** True… although it's more expensive.
- **Laura:** Yes, but you'd need to pay for transportation if you live in the Greenfield neighbourhood.
- **Anna:** Do you think Rosewood is a safe neighbourhood?
- **Laura:** Yes, definitely. My friend lives there, and it's very safe.
- **Anna:** Greenfield is a bit dangerous, isn't it?
- **Laura:** Well… a little, yes. Sometimes things happen.
- **Anna:** Yes, Rosewood is a nicer neighbourhood, but Greenfield has lots of green spaces for walking, running, exercising…
- **Laura:** True, but you can't have everything in one neighbourhood.
- **Anna:** You're right. Thanks, Laura.

1. Answer the following questions about your neighborhood:

• Is it very far from the center?

_____

• What do you like most about your neighbourhood?

_____

• What don't you like about your neighbourhood?

_____

• What are the neighbours like in the neighbourhood?

_____

• Are there good shops and restaurants in your neighbourhood?

_____

2. Describe a neighbourhood that you know and like. Explain why you would like to live in that neighbourhood:

_____

_____

_____

_____

_____

_____

_____

_____

_____

LIKES & DISLIKES

▶ CONVERSATION 1

— **Michael:** Do you like Japanese restaurants?

— **Emily:** Not really. I'm vegetarian, and I prefer to eat at home.

— **Michael:** Don't you like going out to eat at restaurants?

— **Emily:** It depends. I love cooking, and I usually eat at home with my boyfriend.

— **Michael:** Is he vegetarian too?

— **Emily:** No, he likes meat and fish, but he doesn't cook it at home because he knows I don't like it.

— **Michael:** What's your favorite dish?

— **Emily:** I really love potato omelette. I also love pasta with mushrooms and tomatoes.

— **Michael:** Do you like all vegetables?

— **Emily:** Not all of them. I really don't like celery. I'm also not a big fan of cabbage.

— **Michael:** Honestly, I hate carrots.

— **Emily:** Really? I love them.

▶ CONVERSATION 2

- **Clara:** I love your skirt, is it new?
- **Lucy:** No, it's from last year. Are you into fashion?
- **Clara:** Yes, a little. I like going to second-hand stores, and I also enjoy reading fashion magazines.
- **Lucy:** Then you'll like my sister. She loves that kind of stuff too.
- **Clara:** Well, you'll have to introduce me to your sister. Honestly, I hate shopping alone. I prefer going with someone else. I love exchanging opinions about clothes I like.
- **Lucy:** Sure, let's plan something for next week, and I'll introduce you to her.

EXERCISES

1. Write a sentence about the following topics using the verbs "like", "love", "hate", "interest" and "detest".

- Food

_____

- Drink

_____

- Music

_____

- A person

_____

- A film

_____

- A city

_____

- A book

_____

2. React to these statements using: "Me too/Me neither, I do/ I don't"

- I like to eat meat.

  _____

- I hate classical music.

  _____

- I love motorcycles.

  _____

- I don't like beaches.

  _____

- I hate TV series.

  _____

- I like tea more than coffee.

  _____

- I don't like reading.

  _____

THE FAMILY

▶ CONVERSATION 1

— **Gerald:** My family is actually a bit unusual.

— **Alice:** Why do you say that?

— **Gerald:** My father, for example, has only one brother, but he has 8 nephews and nieces.

— **Alice:** Does your uncle have 8 children?

— **Gerald:** Yes, it's not very common these days, don't you think?

— **Alice:** No, not really.

— **Gerald:** And my mother has 4 sisters, and each sister has two daughters, except for my mother, who has two sons.

— **Alice:** Wow! So, how many cousins do you have in total?

— **Gerald:** Well, 8 cousins from my uncle and 8 cousins from my aunts. That's 16 cousins in total.

— **Alice:** Are your grandparents still alive?

— **Gerald:** Yes, all 4 of my grandparents live in Valencia. They're all over 90 years old.

— **Alice:** Yeah, you have a family that's not very conventional.

▶ CONVERSATION 2

- **Olivia:** I don't like family gatherings.
- **Anna:** There's always some drama, right?
- **Olivia:** Yes, all the time. My brother-in-law, Philip, is really difficult. He loves talking about politics and always argues with my nephew, who's very young.
- **Anna:** I get it. When I go to my in-laws' house, it's the same thing.
- **Olivia:** Yeah, and on top of that, my brother's girlfriend is divorced, and my father doesn't like that.
- **Anna:** Your dad is a bit old-fashioned, isn't he?
- **Olivia:** Yes, very much so, and my mother always tries to defend my brother.
- **Anna:** Well, every family has its problems.

EXERCISES

1. **Write the appropriate answer:**

- Your son's son is your…

- Your father's father is your...

- Your uncle's son is your...

- Your mother's sister is your...

- The son of your parents is your…

- Your sister's daughter is your…

---

2. What is your family like? Describe some of your family members, highlighting your relationship with them.

_____

_____

_____

_____

_____

_____

_____

_____

_____

RECOMMENDATIONS

▶ CONVERSATION 1

— **Rita:** Honestly, I don't know what to do with the kids this weekend.

— **Manuela:** There's a really good movie at the cinema that I'd recommend. It's called *The Explorers Club*, and my kids love it.

— **Rita:** That sounds interesting.

— **Manuela:** Yes, but if I were you, I'd go to the 2 p.m. showing because at 4:30 p.m., there are way too many kids.

— **Rita:** Got it. Which cinema is it at?

— **Manuela:** It's at the shopping mall, but I wouldn't recommend driving—it's really hard to find parking. The best thing is to take the train and walk 5 minutes to the cinema.

— **Rita:** Thanks so much, Manuela. I think I'll go this Saturday with the kids.

▶ CONVERSATION 2

- **Sophia:** I need a gift for my father. His birthday is tomorrow, and I still don't have anything.
- **James:** You should buy something today.
- **Sophia:** Yes, but I don't know what.
- **James:** You don't have much time... I recommend a classic gift: a book, a belt, or a bottle of wine.
- **Sophia:** Yes, my father loves red wine.
- **James:** Then you should go to The Wine Cellar, it's a store that has many types of wine.
- **Sophia:** I don't know anything about wine, can you recommend something?
- **James:** The best choice is to buy a classic wine.
- **Sophia:** A Rioja, for example?
- **James:** That's a good option. I also like Ribera del Duero, it's very good.
- **Sophia:** Thank you very much for your recommendation, James.

EXERCISES

1. Make recommendations to these people:

- I want to watch a funny movie.

  _____

- I need a plan for Sunday with my little son.

  _____

- It's my mother's birthday and I don't know what to give her.

  _____

- I'm out of shape and I want to lose weight.

  _____

- I have a headache and a slight fever.

  _____

- I want to impress my girlfriend on our anniversary.

  _____

2. Imagine you have to recommend a vacation spot for your friend. Recommend where to go, where to stay, what to do, etc.

_____

_____

_____

_____

_____

_____

_____

_____

_____

AT THE RESTAURANT

— **Waiter:** Good evening!

— **Diner 1:** Good evening!

— **Waiter:** Do you have a reservation?

— **Diner 1:** Yes, a reservation under the name of Alex Johnson.

— **Waiter:** Yes, a table for two at half past nine. This way, please.

— **Diner 1:** Thank you!

— **Waiter:** Here is the menu.

— **Diners 1 and 2:** Thank you.

— **Waiter:** What would you like to order?

— **Diner 1:** For the starter, a mixed salad for me, please.

— **Diner 2:** For me, vegetable soup.

— **Waiter:** And for the main course?

— **Diner 1:** Seafood rice for two.

— **Waiter:** And to drink?

— **Diner 1:** Wine, please.

— **Waiter:** White or red?

— **Diner 2:** White. And a bottle of water.

— **Waiter:** Cold or room temperature?

— **Diner 2:** Room temperature, please. And still, no gas.

— **Waiter:** Anything else?

— **Diner 1:** No, nothing else for now, thank you.

[Later] …

- **Waiter:** Would you like to have dessert?
- **Diner 1:** Yes, could you bring the dessert menu, please?
- **Waiter:** Here it is.
- **Diner 2:** For me, rice pudding, please.
- **Diner 1:** I'll have the chocolate cake.
- **Waiter:** Anything else? Coffee? Tea?
- **Diner 2:** A cortado for me and a coffee with milk for her.

...

- **Waiter:** Was everything to your liking?
- **Diner 2:** Everything was excellent.
- **Diner 1:** Delicious. Could you bring us the check, please?
- **Waiter:** Will you be paying by card or in cash?
- **Diner 1:** In cash.
- **Waiter:** That will be $97,50.
- **Diner 1:** Here you go. Thank you very much.
- **Waiter:** Thank you both. Have a great evening!
- **Diner 1:** Goodbye!
- **Diner 2:** Bye!

1. **After reading the dialogue, answer true or false in each case.**

- They will have vegetarian dishes for starters.

_____

- For the second course, both of them choose the same dish.

_____

- They do not drink alcohol during the meal.

_____

- Diners like the food.

_____

- Diners pay with a credit card.

_____

2. Write the name of 7 fruits, 7 types of fish, 7 types of meat and 7 different drinks:

- Fruit

- Fish

- Meat

- Drinks

THE WEATHER

▶ **CONVERSATION 1**

— **Carlos:** Normally, in the South of England, it's neither too hot nor too cold.
— **Sophie:** That's true, but it rains a lot, doesn't it?
— **Carlos:** Yes, for example, it's raining now, but tomorrow it will be sunny.
— **Sophie:** Do you think so?
— **Carlos:** Yes, it will be sunny and warm, at least 23 degrees.
— **Sophie:** Well, today it's cold and quite windy.
— **Carlos:** It's very cloudy today, but the weather changes a lot here in just 24 hours.

▶ CONVERSATION 2

- **Emma:** I love it here. The weather is always nice.
- **James:** Yes, the sky is blue almost all year round.
- **Emma:** Sometimes there are storms, and it gets a bit humid, but in general, it's very sunny, and the winter is very mild.
- **James:** The good thing is that if you want to see snow, the mountains aren't too far away.
- **Emma:** Yes, you can go to Sierra Nevada. In winter, it's really cold, and it snows a lot there.
- **James:** Yes, it's a very dry cold over there.

EXERCISES

1. Describe what the weather is generally like in these places:

- In your city/town in the spring.

  _____

  _____

- In the Sahara desert in the summer.

  _____

  _____

- In London in the autumn.

  _____

  _____

- In Moscow in winter.

  _____

  _____

2. Describe what the weather is like today, and make a different prediction for tomorrow.

_____

_____

_____

_____

_____

_____

_____

_____

_____

_____

AT WORK

▶ CONVERSATION 1

- **Sophie:** Do you know what time the meeting is?
- **Emma:** Yes, this afternoon at 3:30 PM.
- **Sophie:** Can you send me an email with the details?
- **Emma:** Yes, no problem. I'll send it to you right away.
- **Sophie:** Are the sales manager and the HR director also going?
- **Emma:** I think so, but they need to confirm before 11 AM.
- **Sophie:** I'm a bit nervous.
- **Emma:** Why? You have a lot of experience.
- **Sophie:** Yes, but the company's financial results aren't great, and they're going to ask a lot of questions.
- **Emma:** But you're not responsible for the financial results.
- **Sophie:** No, but I need to have answers to all their questions.
- **Emma:** Do you need help with the preparation?
- **Sophie:** Yes, please. Would you mind?
- **Emma:** Not at all. I don't have much work this morning, so we can practice.
- **Sophie:** Thank you so much.

▶ CONVERSATION 2

— **James:** Do you like your job?
— **Daniel:** Yes, I like it a lot. The office is very big, and my colleagues are really nice and friendly.
— **James:** And what do you do on a normal workday?
— **Daniel:** Well, the first thing I do is check my emails. Then, we always have a meeting at 10 AM to discuss the day's plan. After that, I work on the computer until lunchtime.
— **James:** And in the afternoon?
— **Daniel:** In the afternoons, we go out to visit clients or make phone calls to talk to them.
— **James:** Is there anything negative about your job?
— **Daniel:** Well, the salary isn't very high in the first year, but it gets better later.
— **James:** Would you recommend your company as a place to work?
— **Daniel:** Yes, but you also have to work hard.
— **James:** Of course, that's normal.

EXERCISES

1. Write the name of the profession.

- I work in a restaurant and serve tables.

_____

- I work in a store and serve customers.

_____

- I work in a restaurant and I cook.

_____

- I teach History at a school.

_____

- I cut and style my clients' hair.

_____

- I work in a hospital and take care of sick patients.

_____

2. Describe the following professions as in the previous exercise.

- Lawyer

_____

_____

_____

- Mechanic

_____

_____

_____

- Firefighter

_____

_____

_____

CITES

▶ CONVERSATION 1

— **Lily:** Next week we're going to Chicago.

— **Ethan:** On vacation?

— **Lily:** Yes, just for three days, but we want to see the city.

— **Ethan:** I know Chicago quite well. My cousins live there.

— **Lily:** Oh, really?

— **Ethan:** Yes, I recommend visiting Millennium Park and the Art Institute in the morning. In the afternoon, there are a lot of tourists, and the lines can be long.

— **Lily:** And for food?

— **Ethan:** You have many options, but I like a restaurant near the river. It's called The Waterhouse, and it has a beautiful view of the skyline.

— **Lily:** There's also a historic district, right?

— **Ethan:** Yes, it's called Old Town, and it's very charming. My cousins live nearby, next to a famous theater.

— **Lily:** The Chicago Theatre?

— **Ethan:** No, that one is downtown. But it's also beautiful, and nearby, there's a plaza with a fountain in the middle. The area is full of cafés and restaurants.

▶ CONVERSATION 2

— **Sophia:** Do you like living in Hong Kong?

— **Leo:** Well, I didn't at first, but now I really like it.

— **Sophia:** What's the city like?

— **Leo:** There are a lot of people, but the city isn't very big. It has different islands and lots of skyscrapers.

— **Sophia:** Is there a subway?

— **Leo:** Yes, the transportation is very good. There's a subway, buses, boats, and taxis aren't very expensive.

— **Sophia:** Yeah, but the traffic…

— **Leo:** Yes, traffic is a problem, like in almost all big cities.

— **Sophia:** It's a great city for shopping, isn't it?

— **Leo:** You're very well-informed! You can find everything there. There are all kinds of shops, and they stay open at night, too.

— **Sophia:** Are there many green spaces?

— **Leo:** It depends. Not many in the city center, but nearby there are some really nice areas for walking. You can also go to the bech—it's very close.

EXERCISES

1. Think about your city or a place you know well and answer the following questions.

- Is it a large, small or medium-sized city? How many inhabitants does it have?

_____

- What are the most famous buildings or monuments?

_____

- What is the city's climate like?

_____

- Is it near the sea?

_____

- Is she famous for some reason?

_____

- Is it an expensive city compared to the rest of the country?

_____

2. Think of a city you like and describe what it is like and what there is in it.

_____

_____

_____

_____

_____

_____

_____

_____

_____

_____

_____

_____

IN THE TAXI

▶ CONVERSATION 1

- **Taxi Driver:** Good morning!
- **Passenger:** Can you take me to the airport, please?
- **Taxi Driver:** Of course. Which terminal?
- **Passenger:** Terminal 4.
- **Taxi Driver:** Departures, right?
- **Passenger:** Yes, please.
- **Taxi Driver:** Are you going on vacation?
- **Passenger:** No, it's a business trip to New York.
- **Taxi Driver:** My brother lives in New York.
- **Passenger:** It's a very interesting city, isn't it?
- **Taxi Driver:** Yes, I like it a lot.

(…)

- **Taxi Driver:** Well, here we are at Terminal 4. That'll be $42.60.
- **Passenger:** Here's $45.
- **Taxi Driver:** Do you need a receipt?
- **Passenger:** Yes, please.
- **Taxi Driver:** No problem.

▶ CONVERSATION 2

- **Passenger:** To the train station, please.
- **Taxi Driver:** Union Station?
- **Passenger:** Yes, please.
- **Taxi Driver:** Do you want to put your suitcase in the trunk?
- **Passenger:** No, thank you. It's not very big.
- **Taxi Driver:** You're not from the U.S., are you?
- **Passenger:** No, I'm Brazilian.
- **Taxi Driver:** Oh, Brazil is a beautiful country.
- **Passenger:** Yes, but I'm in the U.S. for business.
- **Taxi Driver:** Do you like it here?
- **Passenger:** Yes, but this isn't my first time visiting. I come here regularly.
- **Taxi Driver:** My friend is in Rio de Janeiro on vacation right now.
- **Passenger:** Rio is a very popular destination for tourists.
- **Taxi Driver:** You don't like it?
- **Passenger:** Honestly, I've never been to Rio.

(…)

- **Taxi Driver:** Here we are at Union Station. That'll be $18.75.
- **Passenger:** Thank you very much. Can you give me a receipt?
- **Taxi Driver:** Of course!

EXERCISES

1. Complete the following dialogue in a taxi.

- Are you from San Francisco?

_____

- Do you like the city?

_____

- Are you here for a visit or for work?

_____

- It's 29 euros and 25. Do you need an invoice?

_____

- Thank you very much and have a nice day.

_____

2. Indicate which of the following words are related to taxis and which are not.

- Window
- Bottle
- Taximeter
- Tree
- Free
- Occupied
- Table
- Seat

- Steering wheel
- Driver Lamp
- Brake
- Rearview mirror
- Wall
- Trunk
- Cupboard
- Rearview mirror

MUSIC

▶ CONVERSATION 1

— **Julian:** My brother wants to study music at the conservatory.
— **Rachel:** Your brother is really talented at music.
— **Julian:** Yes, he plays the piano and the guitar really well. Now he's learning to play the violin.
— **Rachel:** Honestly, I admire your brother.
— **Julian:** Me too. I don't have any musical talent—I'm really bad.
— **Rachel:** That's not true, you sing really well.
— **Julian:** Well, a little, I guess. I sing in the choir, but I can't play any instruments.
— **Rachel:** I can play the piano a little, but not like your brother, of course.
— **Julian:** Do you prefer playing classical or modern music?
— **Rachel:** I prefer playing modern music.
— **Julian:** My brother prefers classical music, but a lot of people think it's boring.
— **Rachel:** Well, it depends.
— **Julian:** My brother's favorite composer is Bach.
— **Rachel:** I like Bach too, but I can't play any of his pieces on the piano. It's a bit too hard for me.

▶ CONVERSATION 2

—   **Edith:** You have to listen to this band. There are 3 guys and 2 girls, and their concerts are so much fun.
—   **Mandy:** What kind of music do they play?
—   **Edith:** It's a mix of styles, and they play a lot of instruments: guitar, bass, drums, accordion, piano, and sometimes they do electronic music.
—   **Mandy:** Hmm, I don't know. I prefer more traditional music. I love Julio Iglesias.
—   **Edith:** Do you like romantic music?
—   **Mandy:** Yes, I love romantic singers and ballads.
—   **Edith:** But all their songs sound the same, don't they?
—   **Mandy:** Haha! No, I think today's pop music is very similar and not very interesting.
—   **Edith:** We definitely have different tastes in music.

1. Answer the following questions about music.

● What types of music do you like the most?

_____

● Do you know how to play any instruments?

_____

● How and where do you usually listen to music?

_____

● Do you have a favorite band or singer?

_____

● Do you like going to concerts?

_____

● Do you like to work or study with music?

_____

2. Complete the following dialogue about music.

- I especially like it in the morning when I have breakfast.

_____

- Generally classical music, but sometimes something more current.

_____

- The guitar and the piano, but I haven't played for a long time.

_____

- Mozart and Beethoven.

_____

- No, my wife prefers Latin music.

_____

STUGIES

▶ CONVERSATION 1

— **Martina:** The exams are next week.

— **Mariana:** I'm so nervous!

— **Martina:** Yeah, for me, the hardest ones are Math and Physics.

— **Mariana:** Really? For me, History and Philosophy are the worst.

— **Martina:** French and Art are the easiest subjects, right?

— **Mariana:** Yes, and P.E. too.

— **Martina:** Well, I'm not as good as you at sports.

— **Mariana:** I have an idea.

— **Martina:** What?

— **Mariana:** Why don't we study together for the exams? I can help you with numbers.

— **Martina:** And I'm the top student in History class.

— **Mariana:** Perfect!

▶ CONVERSATION 2

— **Max:** Honestly, I still don't know what I want to study at university.

— **John:** Well, you don't have much time left.

— **Max:** I know. What about you?

— **John:** I'm very clear about it. I'm going to study Economics, like my sister.

— **Max:** You have to study a lot, don't you?

— **John:** Of course, but you always have to work hard at university.

— **Max:** I'm not sure if I even want to go to university.

— **John:** Are you serious? You always get great grades in English, and you really enjoy language classes.

— **Max:** I think I need a gap year before going to university. I want to travel and work in other countries.

— **John:** Oh, that's not a bad idea!

EXERCISES

1. Write the name of 8 subjects that are studied at school.

1. _____

2. _____

3. _____

4. _____

5. _____

6. _____

7. _____

8. _____

2. Complete the following dialogue about studies.

- Really? For me, math and physics are the hardest.

  _____

- I usually study alone in my room with some music.

  _____

- In my case, the easiest ones are Art and Geography.

  _____

- Martha the art teacher. She is very good.

  _____

- Mr. Martin the math teacher because he is very boring.

  _____

AT THE AIRPORT

▶ CONVERSATION 1

- **Emma:** What time does the plane leave?
- **Lily:** At 3, but the boarding gates open at 2:15.
- **Emma:** Okay, we have time to check in our luggage and grab a coffee.
- **Lily:** Yes, but first we have to go through security, and sometimes it takes a long time.
- **Emma:** How long is the flight?
- **Lily:** Just two hours.
- **Emma:** But in New York, it's one hour earlier, right?
- **Lily:** Yes, we have to set our clocks back one hour.
- **Emma:** Are you afraid of flying?
- **Lily:** I'm not scared, but I don't really like it.
- **Emma:** For me, the worst part is the airport: transportation, lines, luggage, stress, etc.

▶ CONVERSATION 2

— **Agent:** May I see your passports, please?

— **Passenger:** Yes, here they are.

— **Agent:** How many people are traveling with you?

— **Passenger:** My husband and my two children. There are four of us in total.

— **Agent:** How many suitcases do you have?

— **Passenger:** Three large suitcases, two backpacks, and a carry-on bag.

— **Agent:** Okay, you can check in the three suitcases and one backpack if you'd like.

— **Passenger:** No, we'd prefer to keep the backpacks with us.

— **Agent:** The flight is completely full, and we recommend checking in the backpacks.

— **Passenger:** Well, in that case, we'll check in one.

— **Agent:** Very good. Here are your tickets. Boarding is at 6 at Gate 12.

— **Passenger:** Thank you.

1. Write the name of 5 things that you can find in all airports, and 5 things that are on all airplanes.

1. _____

2. _____

3. _____

4. _____

5. _____

1. _____

2. _____

3. _____

4. _____

5. _____

2. **Complete the following dialogue at an airport.**

- What time does our flight leave?

_____

- Do you know which boarding gate is?

_____

- Is it allowed to go through security with a bottle of water and a snack?

_____

- Window or aisle? Do you have a preference?

_____

- Do you have a routine when you travel by plane?

_____

- Do you get nervous when taking off or landing?

_____

BOOKS

- **Olivia:** The trip is a bit long, but I don't mind because I have a really interesting book.
- **Sophia:** Oh, really? What's it about?
- **Olivia:** It's a 19th-century novel. It describes the relationship between parents and children and the differences in the way each generation thinks.
- **Sophia:** Is it very long?
- **Olivia:** No, it's a short novel.
- **Sophia:** I don't really like reading fiction. I prefer other kinds of books.
- **Olivia:** Like what?
- **Sophia:** I read a lot of current affairs magazines, and I love reading biographies of people I find interesting.
- **Olivia:** What are you reading now?
- **Sophia:** It's a book about the life of Audrey Hepburn.
- **Olivia:** And is it interesting?
- **Sophia:** I'm really enjoying it, and there are some fascinating chapters about her life in Belgium and Hollywood.
- **Olivia:** Is that the book you have in your bag?
- **Sophia:** Yes, it's a bit long, but very easy to read.
- **Olivia:** It looks huge! How many pages does it have?
- **Sophia:** Almost 700, but the writing is very clear, so you can read it quickly.
- **Olivia:** Okay, I'll read it after I finish mine.

EXERCISES

1. Answer the following questions about the books.

- What kind of books do you like to read?

_____

- Do you have a favorite book?

_____

- Where do you usually buy books?

_____

- Can you name 4 genres of books?

_____

- What is the difference between a library and a bookstore?

_____

- How many books do you think you have in your house?

_____

2. Think of a book you know and describe the story in a simple and brief way.

_____

_____

_____

_____

_____

SHOPPING

▶ CONVERSATION 1

— **Ethan:** This store has really good clothes.

— **Lily:** Yes, look at that white shirt. It's perfect for your blue jacket.

— **Ethan:** I'm going to try it on.

— **Lily:** It looks great on you.

— **Ethan:** Yeah, I really like it too.

— **Lily:** Let's go pay.

— **Cashier:** That'll be $65. Card or cash?

— **Ethan:** Card, please.

— **Cashier:** Sorry, we don't accept AmeriPay.

— **Ethan:** Then I think I'll need to withdraw some cash. Is there an ATM nearby?

— **Lily:** Wait, you can use my card.

— **Ethan:** If you don't mind…

— **Lily:** No, of course not.

— **Cashier:** Would you like a bag?

— **Ethan:** No, thanks, I already have one.

— **Cashier:** Thank you very much. Have a great day!

CONVERSATION 2

— **Hannah:** Let's go into this shoe store. I want to check out some boots for winter.
— **Jack:** I also need to buy some black shoes for work.
— **Hannah:** Wow, everything is really expensive, isn't it?
— **Jack:** Yeah, I think we can find something cheaper in another store.
— **Hannah:** We could go to Emily's shop. We always find things we like there.
— **Jack:** They have a lot of coats, pants, and sweaters, but they don't sell shoes.
— **Hannah:** That's true.
— **Jack:** What if we try the Grandview Mall?
— **Hannah:** I don't really like it. The stores there are cheap, but not very good. The quality of the clothes is low, and the staff isn't very friendly.
— **Jack:** What about the shoe store on Madison Street?
— **Hannah:** The one next to the sports shop?
— **Jack:** Yeah, where you bought your heels for your cousin's wedding.
— **Hannah:** Oh yeah, they have good shoes, and the prices are reasonable.
— **Jack:** Let's go, then!

EXERCISES

1. Write the name of 3 things that you can buy in each of these stores:

- A clothing store.

_____

- A fruit shop.

_____

- A stationery store.

_____

- An electronics store.

_____

- A drugstore.

_____

- A furniture store.

_____

2. Answer the following questions on the topic of shopping.

- What is the difference between "going shopping" and "doing the shopping"?

  _____

- What are the ways you can pay in a store?

  _____

- What is the name of the person who works in a clothing store?

  _____

- What do the letters S, M, L and XL refer to on a piece of clothing?

  _____

- Where can you buy plants and flowers?

  _____

- What is the difference between a shopping mall and a super-market?

  _____

AT THE HOTEL

▶ CONVERSATION 1

- **Customer:** Good morning! I have a reservation under the name Daniel Carter.
- **Receptionist:** Good morning, Mr. Carter! A reservation for three days, correct?
- **Customer:** Yes, a double room for three days.
- **Receptionist:** Would you prefer a room with a view of the pool or the garden?
- **Customer:** Don't you have any rooms with an ocean view?
- **Receptionist:** No, I'm sorry, they're all booked. During the summer, the hotel is fully occupied.
- **Customer:** Then I'll take the garden view, please. It's quieter.
- **Receptionist:** Here is your key. It's room 309, on the third floor. The elevator is to your left.
- **Customer:** What time is breakfast?
- **Receptionist:** Between 7 AM and 10 AM.
- **Customer:** We have two very heavy suitcases. Could someone help us take them to the room?
- **Receptionist:** Of course! I'll send someone right away.

▶ CONVERSATION 2

— **Receptionist:** Thank you for staying at the Ocean View Hotel.
— **Customer:** Honestly, I will never stay at this hotel again.
— **Receptionist:** Did you have any issues?
— **Customer:** Yes, quite a few.
— **Receptionist:** I'm very sorry, ma'am. Is there anything we can do?
— **Customer:** I'm very unhappy with the room. The air conditioning doesn't work, so we have to keep the window open at night, but there's too much noise from the street. The water in the shower is either too hot or too cold. Also, the food quality at the restaurant is really low.
— **Receptionist:** Ma'am, I'll speak to the manager, and he will contact you as soon as possible.
— **Customer:** Thank you. I expect some compensation for all this.
— **Receptionist:** We sincerely apologize.

EXERCISES

1. Write the name of 5 things you can find in a hotel room.

1. _____

2. _____

3. _____

4. _____

5. _____

2. Complete each sentence with a word to make the sentence make sense.

1. Good morning! I have a _____ for a double room for 2 days.

2. At this moment the _____ is not working and you have to use the stairs.

3. The room has _____ to the pool.

4. The cafeteria opens at 7 in the morning for _____.

5. Can you tell me what the _____ of the wi-fi is?

ANIMALS

▶ CONVERSATION 1

- **Emma:** My nephew loves going to the zoo.
- **Ryan:** That makes sense; kids really enjoy seeing animals. My son is fascinated by monkeys and elephants.
- **Emma:** Yes, but I think my nephew's favorites are the penguins.
- **Ryan:** I remember the penguins well—they're next to the tigers and lions, right?
- **Emma:** Personally, I really like giraffes and hippos.
- **Ryan:** I love pandas.
- **Emma:** We should go together one day. There's a dolphin show every weekend.
- **Ryan:** Great idea!

▶ CONVERSATION 2

- **Jake:** I really like animals, but I live in a small apartment and can't have a dog.
- **Sophie:** I also live in an apartment, but I have a cat named Milo.
- **Jake:** My friend has a turtle, a bird, and a fish at home.
- **Sophie:** Wow, that's a lot!
- **Jake:** Yeah, but he lives in a house in the countryside, and his dad has cows, sheep, chickens, horses, and more.
- **Sophie:** With so many animals, it must be hard to go on vacation!.

EXERCISES

1. Write the names of the animals above their description.

_____

- It has four legs and lots of fur. It is man's best friend.

_____

- They are small felines. They like to hunt mice and are independent.

_____

- They are very tall animals with enormous necks. They live in Africa.

_____

- They are large, very calm animals that eat grass. They produce milk.

_____

- It is a yellow and black insect. It can fly and makes honey.

2. Now describe the following animals.

- A horse.

  _____

- A whale.

  _____

- A bear.

  _____

- A sheep

  _____

- A snake

  _____

- A lion

  _____

DIRECTIONS

▶ CONVERSATION 1

— **Tourist:** Excuse me, do you know how to get to Maple Square?

— **Local:** Hmm, I'm not sure. Sorry.

— **Tourist:** Thanks anyway.

— **Local:** Wait… Yes, I remember now! Maple Square is next to Greenway Park.

— **Tourist:** Can I walk there?

— **Local:** Yes, it's not too far. About 15 minutes or so.

— **Tourist:** In which direction?

— **Local:** You need to go straight until you reach that church, then turn left.

— **Tourist:** Straight to the church, then left.

— **Local:** Yes, and after that, you have to cross the street and…

— **Tourist:** Yes?

— **Local:** I don't remember if you need to turn left or right. It's best to ask again.

— **Tourist:** Got it. Thank you very much.

▶ CONVERSATION 2

— **Receptionist:** Hello, good afternoon!

— **Tourist:** Good afternoon! We'd like to visit the Film Museum.

— **Receptionist:** It's in the north part of the city.

— **Tourist:** Is it possible to walk there?

— **Receptionist:** No, it's too far. The best option is to take the subway.

— **Tourist:** Which stop should we get off at?

— **Receptionist:** The closest stop is Main Street Station.

— **Tourist:** Which subway line should we take?

— **Receptionist:** There's a subway entrance to the left of the hotel. You need to take the blue line and then transfer to the yellow line.

— **Tourist:** Always heading north, right?

— **Receptionist:** Exactly. It takes about 30 minutes.

— **Tourist:** Great, thank you very much!

EXERCISES

1. Complete the sentences with the correct word:

1. Turn to _____ and then to the left.

2. Continue _____ until the end of the street.

3. The square is very _____. Just 5 minutes walk.

4. Do you know where the subway _____ is?

5. You have to _____ to the left and then cross the street.

2. Complete the following dialogue between a tourist and a local person.

• The train station? Yes, I know the area.

_____

• No, it is very close, there is no need to take a taxi.

_____

• Yes, you have to turn right first and then left.

_____

• No, it is not necessary to cross the street.

_____

• About 5 minutes from here.

_____

CHARACTER

▶ CONVERSATION 1

— **Emma:** You have four siblings, right?

— **Jake:** Yes, there are five of us in total, and we're all very different.

— **Emma:** Really?

— **Jake:** My oldest sister is very serious and organized. She likes to be in control and has a strong personality.

— **Emma:** And the rest?

— **Jake:** My sister Olivia is the second oldest, and she's very independent. She doesn't like big groups and is a little shy. Daniel is the third, and he's really funny. He loves to talk and joke around with us.

— **Emma:** And your youngest brother?

— **Jake:** Noah is the most social one. He's very outgoing and cheerful. He loves music and sings with a group of friends.

— **Emma:** And what about you?

— **Jake:** Compared to them, I'm very calm and laid-back. I'm not as hardworking as they are—I just enjoy spending time with my friends, eating, and talking for hours.

▶ CONVERSATION 2

— **Sophia:** Mom and dad are really different, don't you think?

— **Lily:** Yeah, totally different.

— **Sophia:** Mom is very sweet and kind. She's always in a good mood, and she loves cooking for everyone and doing things for others.

— **Lily:** Yeah, dad is great too, but he's stricter and his mood changes a lot. Sometimes he's happy, and sometimes he's sad.

— **Sophia:** Yeah, mom is more emotionally stable.

— **Lily:** Yes, and more social. She loves to talk and spends hours on the phone with family.

— **Sophia:** On the other hand, dad is more reserved and a bit quiet.

— **Lily:** Yeah, but sometimes mom can be a little loud, right?

— **Sophia:** Yeah, but I think I'm more like dad.

— **Lily:** Yeah, I think so too.

EXERCISES

1. Write the adjective above each definition:

_____

- He is a person who does not talk much and likes to be silent.

_____

- He is very sociable and communicative. He always likes to be with people.

_____

- She almost never smiles and doesn't like to joke.

_____

- She loves helping other people and is very polite.

_____

- He is too relaxed and does not like to work or exercise.

2. Think of two people you know with very different personalities and describe them.

_____

_____

_____

_____

_____

IN THE CAFETERIA

▶ CONVERSATION 1

— **Liam:** I think I'll have a black coffee. What about you?

— **Sophie:** A latte. I don't like black coffee.

— **Liam:** Besides, it's really hot today. I think I'll have an iced black coffee.

— **Sophie:** I prefer coffee when it's hot, even in warm weather. And I also like it with sugar.

— **Liam:** I usually drink it without sugar, but sometimes I add a little.

— **Sophie:** Do you want something to eat?

— **Liam:** I feel like something sweet.

— **Sophie:** How about toast with jam and butter?

— **Liam:** Hmm… What if we share a piece of chocolate cake?

— **Sophie:** Of course! I can never say no to chocolate cake.

— **Liam:** *Haha!* Me neither!

▶ CONVERSATION 2

- **Waiter:** Good afternoon! What can I get you?
- **Customer 1:** I'll have an espresso with a little milk and a bottle of mineral water.
- **Customer 2:** Do you have fresh juices?
- **Waiter:** We have freshly squeezed orange juice.
- **Customer 2:** Nothing else?
- **Waiter:** We have bottled apple and pineapple juice.
- **Customer 2:** Then I'll take the fresh orange juice.
- **Waiter:** Perfect.

(Later...)

- **Customer 1:** Excuse me! Can I get the check, please?
- **Customer 2:** No, no, I'll pay this time.
- **Customer 1:** You can pay next time. This one's on me.
- **Waiter:** That'll be $9.50.
- **Customer 1:** Here you go.
- **Waiter:** Do you have a smaller bill?
- **Customer 1:** No, I only have this $50 bill.
- **Customer 2:** I have a $10 bill.
- **Waiter:** If you don't mind, that would be much better.
- **Customer 2:** Alright, I'll pay this time.
- **Customer 1:** Well... okay then.

EXERCISES

1. Complete the following dialogue in a cafeteria between the waiter and the customer.

- What would you like to drink?

  _____

- Something to eat?

  _____

- No, we only have it with cream.

  _____

- In total it is 17 dollars, please.

  _____

- The bathrooms are at the back on the left.

  _____

2. Write 5 things you can normally drink and eat in a cafe.

1. _____	1. _____
2. _____	2. _____
3. _____	3. _____
4. _____	4. _____
5. _____	5. _____

SERIES

▶ CONVERSATION 1

— **Emma:** I'm obsessed with a TV show.

— **Chloe:** Which one?

— **Emma:** It's called Special Mission.

— **Chloe:** What's it about?

— **Emma:** It's about a group of women who work for a secret agency and have to travel around the world capturing criminals.

— **Chloe:** So, you like action series, right?

— **Emma:** Yes, but this one is different. All the main characters are women, and everything feels very realistic.

— **Chloe:** Is it an American show?

— **Emma:** No, it's British, but there are many scenes in South America and Africa.

— **Chloe:** Are there any famous actresses in it?

— **Emma:** No, but I actually prefer that. I like discovering new actresses instead of seeing the same faces from other shows.

— **Chloe:** How many episodes are there?

— **Emma:** There are only two seasons, and each has ten episodes.

— **Chloe:** Is it very violent?

— **Emma:** Not really, but there are some intense action scenes.

— **Chloe:** I'll watch an episode and let you know if I like it.

▶ CONVERSATION 2

— **Mia:** Do you watch a lot of TV shows, Jake?

— **Jake:** Not really, I'm not watching any shows at the moment.

— **Mia:** You don't like them?

— **Jake:** I do, but I prefer watching movies. TV shows are too long.

— **Mia:** They kind of bore me.

— **Jake:** Really?

— **Mia:** Well, I get bored when people talk about them all the time—characters, actors, and storylines I don't even know.

— **Jake:** Yeah, I get that. It can be a bit much.

— **Mia:** I don't understand why people are so obsessed with TV series. They're not even real.

— **Jake:** So, you're not a fan of fiction?

— **Mia:** I prefer real things. Documentaries and reality shows, for example, are way more interesting to me.

— **Jake:** What kind of documentaries do you like?

— **Mia:** I love biographies of interesting people. I also enjoy cooking shows.

— **Jake:** I see, you're a more practical person.

— **Mia:** Yes, and that's why I don't like spending hours watching fantasy or fictional series.

— **Jake:** Makes sense.

1. Write the correct word above each definition:

_____

- A program that deals with real topics of scientific, social, informative or educational interest.

_____

- A funny and laugh-out-loud movie.

_____

- They are divided into different chapters and there are usually one or two each year.

_____

- Programs that describe a person's life.

_____

- The main character in a story.

2. Think of a series or movie that you like and describe the story in a simple way.

_____

_____

_____

_____

_____

_____

_____

_____

_____

_____

_____

_____

_____

_____

_____

_____

PHYSICAL DESCRIPTION

▶ CONVERSATION 1

— **Adela:** We're looking for a model for the new marketing campaign.
— **Noel:** I'd like to be a model.
— **Adela:** No, no, we're looking for a tall guy.
— **Noel:** But I'm not short.
— **Adela:** You're neither tall nor short. Besides, we prefer someone with dark hair.
— **Noel:** I'm blond, but I can change my hair color.
— **Adela:** Hmm, I think you're a bit overweight now, and we're looking for a slimmer guy.
— **Noel:** Don't you think I'm handsome?
— **Adela:** You're not ugly, Noel, but we want someone different. It's nothing personal.

▶ CONVERSATION 2

— **Nadia:** You have such beautiful eyes, Lucy.
— **Lucy:** Thank you. I'm the only one with green eyes; everyone else in my family has brown eyes.
— **Nadia:** Is your mother Spanish?
— **Lucy:** Yes, she has very dark hair, dark eyes, and tan skin.
— **Nadia:** And your father is English, right?
— **Lucy:** Yes, he has lighter eyes and slightly blond hair, although it's almost white now.
— **Nadia:** Are your parents as tall as you?

— **Lucy:** Yes, but my brothers are much taller than me.

— **Nadia:** You have brothers? I didn't know that.

— **Lucy:** Yes, the oldest one lives in London. He's very tall and slim. He has very short hair and looks a lot like my father.

— **Nadia:** And your other brother?

— **Lucy:** He's tall too, but he looks more like my mother. He has dark, long hair, and a small mouth and nose. He's very popular with the girls.

— **Nadia:** I can imagine.

EXERCISES

1. Complete the sentences with the appropriate adjective.

1. She is a very _____ girl. She is 6 feet tall.

2. Ana is very _____. She doesn't eat much and she exercises a lot.

3. Beatriz is very _____. All the boys are crazy about her.

4. My grandmother is very _____. She is 99 years old.

5. My sister has _____ hair. She used to have it very short.

2. Think of a man and a woman you know and describe them physically.

LOVE

▶ CONVERSATION 1

— **Emily:** I think I'm in love.

— **James:** You're in love? Again?

— **Emily:** Yes, but this time it's different.

— **James:** With whom?

— **Emily:** A guy who works in my office.

— **James:** You work together?

— **Emily:** Yes, and we see each other every day at lunch in the cafeteria.

— **James:** Do you think he feels the same way?

— **Emily:** I don't know, but we talk a lot and have fun together. He's funny and makes me laugh.

— **James:** So, you're not sure if he likes you back?

— **Emily:** I'm not sure, it's hard to tell, but I think he does.

— **James:** Emily, you always say that, and then…

— **Emily:** No, really, this time it's different. I think he's really interested, but he's a little shy.

— **James:** Then why don't you ask him out?

— **Emily:** A date?

— **James:** Yeah, for a drink or dinner.

— **Emily:** Well, there's a small problem.

— **James:** What is it?

— **Emily:** He has a girlfriend.

▶ CONVERSATION 2

— **Ethan:** Olivia, there's something I want to tell you.
— **Olivia:** Ethan, you look a little pale. Are you okay?
— **Ethan:** Nothing, nothing, I just need some water.
— **Olivia:** Well, what do you want to tell me?
— **Ethan:** Well, I… It's just that you… You and I…
— **Olivia:** Are you sure you're okay?
— **Ethan:** Yeah, but there are too many people here. Let's go over there, that bench is empty.
— **Olivia:** Ethan, it's a public park, there are always people here.
— **Ethan:** I need to tell you something in private.
— **Olivia:** Okay, let's go.
— **Ethan:** Olivia, I… I… I think I have feelings for you.
— **Olivia:** What do you mean?
— **Ethan:** Well… We're friends, and well… I like spending time with you.
— **Olivia:** Yeah, I like spending time with my friends too.
— **Ethan:** I mean I like being with you, but not just as a friend.
— **Olivia:** You don't want to be my friend?
— **Ethan:** No, no, no. I want to be your friend, but at the same time, I don't.
— **Olivia:** I'm really confused, Ethan.
— **Ethan:** Yeah, I'm just a little nervous.
— **Olivia:** Why?
— **Ethan:** Because I want to tell you that I'm in love with you, but I don't know how.

EXERCISES

1. Complete the following dialogue between two friends.

- Are you in love? Who is she?

_____

- And what is she like?

_____

- And she knows how you feel?

_____

- Do you think she's interested?

_____

- What are you going to do? Do you have a plan?

_____

2. A friend asks you for advice in the following situations. Write a recommendation for each case.

- I have a first date with a girl tomorrow and I don't know where to go.

_____

_____

- I want to break up with my boyfriend but I don't know how. Should I text him??

_____

_____

- I'm in love with my sister's friend but they don't know anything.

_____

_____

- I have a blind date tonight, do you have any advice?

_____

_____

- Saturday is our first anniversary and I don't have a plan.

_____

_____

HEALTH

▶ CONVERSATION 1

— **Doctor:** Good morning!
— **Patient:** Good morning! I have an appointment for a check-up.
— **Doctor:** I need to ask you a few questions before the physical exam.
— **Patient:** Yes, of course.
— **Doctor:** In general, do you have any pain?
— **Patient:** Sometimes in the afternoons, after eating, I get a headache that lasts a couple of hours.
— **Doctor:** Do you drink coffee?
— **Patient:** Yes, too much.
— **Doctor:** Try to reduce your intake for a few weeks.
— **Patient:** I'll try.
— **Doctor:** Do you smoke?
— **Patient:** No, I don't smoke at all.
— **Doctor:** Do you drink alcohol?
— **Patient:** A glass of wine with dinner, and sometimes a few beers with friends on the weekends.
— **Doctor:** Do you have a balanced diet?
— **Patient:** It depends. Some weeks I don't eat very well because I don't cook much, but I try to have a varied diet.
— **Doctor:** Do you eat a lot of sweets?
— **Patient:** No, but I do eat a lot of fatty foods.
— **Doctor:** Do you exercise?
— **Patient:** I like walking, and once a week, I go running.
— **Doctor:** Thank you.

▶ CONVERSATION 2

— **Emma:** What's wrong? You don't look well.
— **Leo:** Yeah, I don't feel good.
— **Emma:** Does something hurt?
— **Leo:** My stomach hurts.
— **Emma:** I think you ate too much.
— **Leo:** Maybe. I feel a little dizzy.
— **Emma:** Do you want some water with baking soda?
— **Leo:** Yes, please.
— **Emma:** Does anything else hurt?
— **Leo:** No, but I think I'm going to throw up.
— **Emma:** That's probably for the best.
— **Leo:** Yeah, I have indigestion.
— **Emma:** Let's go to the bathroom.
— **Leo:** Thanks for taking care of me, Emma.

1. Write the appropriate body part above its definition:

_____

- You have two and they are on your face.

_____

- They are two limbs that end in hands.

_____

- It is the upper part of the body and the face is in it.

_____

- It is the back of your body. You cannot see it without a mirror.

_____

- You have two and they end at the feet.

2. Recommend a remedy to the following people:

- I've eaten too much and now my stomach hurts.

- I have a terrible headache.

- I have a sore throat and a slight fever. I think I have the flu.

- My back hurts a lot after going to the gym.

- I cut my finger with a knife and it's bleeding quite a bit.

SPORTS

▶ CONVERSATION 1

— **Wyatt:** You're really into sports, aren't you?

— **Savannah:** Yes, I love sports.

— **Wyatt:** I really like team sports: hockey, basketball, rugby, baseball…

— **Savannah:** Honestly, I prefer individual sports: tennis, swimming, track, golf…

— **Wyatt:** Don't you like playing sports with other people?

— **Savannah:** Yes, I do. On weekends, I coach a women's basketball team. It's really fun.

— **Wyatt:** I always need to play sports with friends because I get bored alone. I don't like running or going to the gym.

— **Savannah:** I understand, but it depends on your motivation. When I exercise, I always have goals, and for me, that's a bigger motivation than just working out with friends.

— **Wyatt:** So, you're pretty competitive when it comes to sports, huh?

— **Savannah:** Yes, I love the thrill of competition.

▶ CONVERSATION 2

— **Hudson:** The Olympics start this week!
— **Autumn:** Yes! I love watching sports on TV.
— **Hudson:** I really enjoy the Olympics because they feature sports you don't usually see.
— **Autumn:** That's true! There are events like fencing, rowing, archery, and badminton that you don't often get to watch.
— **Hudson:** My favorites are track and cycling.
— **Autumn:** I love rhythmic gymnastics and swimming.
— **Hudson:** And it's even more exciting because so many countries compete.
— **Autumn:** Exactly! Winning a medal is such a huge honor for an entire country.
— **Hudson:** I agree. It doesn't matter if it's gold, silver, or bronze—if you win an Olympic medal, you'll remember it for the rest of your life.

1. Write the name of each sport above its definition:

_____

- It is played with small yellow or green balls and rackets.

_____

- Each team has 5 players and they are usually very tall. The ball is very big.

_____

- The ball is shaped like a melon and the players are very strong.

_____

- It is a very tough sport and you need a bicycle.

_____

- It is a winter sport that is practiced in the snow. It can be a little dangerous.

2. Now describe the following sports:

- Waterpolo

  _____

  _____

- Swimming

  _____

  _____

- Hockey

  _____

  _____

- Baseball

  _____

  _____

- Boxing

  _____

  _____

AT THE BAR

▶ CONVERSATION 1

— **Waiter:** Good evening… What can I get you?
— **Elliot:** A beer, please.
— **Travis:** Same for me.
— **Waiter:** Bottle or draft?
— **Elliot:** Is the draft beer cold?
— **Waiter:** Yes, it's nice and cold.
— **Elliot:** Then I'll have draft.
— **Travis:** I prefer a bottled beer, please.
— **Waiter:** Coming right up.
— **Travis:** Should we sit at that table?
— **Elliot:** I like staying at the bar. Do you mind?
— **Travis:** No, the bar is fine.
— **Elliot:** Do you feel like having some olives with the beer?
— **Travis:** Yeah, good idea—I'm a bit hungry.
— **Elliot:** Excuse me, could we get some olives, please?
— **Waiter:** Of course. Green or black?
— **Elliot:** Green, please.

(…)

— **Travis:** Excuse me, can we get the check, please?
— **Waiter:** That'll be $17.50.

▶ CONVERSATION 2

— **Landon:** This bar has really good coffee.

— **Milo:** Oh, well, we can have a cup before the concert. We've got time.

— **Landon:** Sounds great!

— **Waiter:** Good afternoon, what can I get you?

— **Landon:** Can you recommend a good coffee?

— **Waiter:** Do you prefer espresso, cappuccino, or an Americano?

— **Landon:** Espresso for me.

— **Milo:** Same here.

— **Waiter:** We have an excellent dark roast espresso with hints of chocolate and caramel. It's $4.50 per cup.

— **Landon:** Do you have single-origin Ethiopian coffee?

— **Waiter:** Yes, we have a fantastic Ethiopian brew. It's a bit pricier, but personally, it's my favorite. $7 per cup.

— **Milo:** I'll have the dark roast espresso.

— **Landon:** I'll try the Ethiopian.

— **Waiter:** Perfect. I'll bring your coffees to the table.

— **Milo:** Could you also bring us a croissant?

— **Waiter:** Of course. Plain or with chocolate?

— **Milo:** Chocolate.

— **Waiter:** Coming right up!

EXERCISES

1. Answer the following questions.

- What is the name of the person who works in a bar?

_____

- What three types of wine do you know depending on their color?

_____

- What is the name of the frozen water that is put in drinks to cool them?

_____

- What is the name of a popular drink in your country?

_____

- What is the name of the liquid extracted from the fruit?

_____

- What can we say to indicate that we want to pay?

_____

2. Complete the sentences with one word.

1. I'm hungry, should we order some green _____ to eat?

2. I'm not going to drink alcohol today. I think I'll have a _____ of sparkling water.

3. If you are hungry I recommend you to eat a _____. Here are really good.

4. I think there is no table service at this bar. We have to order at the _____.

5. They do not accept _____, only card.

AT THE GYM

▶ **CONVERSATION 1**

— **Customer:** Hi! It's my first day, and I don't know my way around the gym.
— **Trainer:** No problem, I can show you around.
— **Customer:** Thank you so much.
— **Trainer:** Over here, we have the treadmills.
— **Customer:** Oh, they look really modern.
— **Trainer:** Yes, everything here is brand new. On this side, we have the free weights.
— **Customer:** I think I need to work on my strength a bit.
— **Trainer:** In this room, we have the yoga and Pilates studio.
— **Customer:** Are there classes every day?
— **Trainer:** Yes, we offer multiple classes in the morning and afternoon.
— **Customer:** And that room over there?
— **Trainer:** That's the other studio, where we hold spinning classes.
— **Customer:** And the locker rooms are over there, right?
— **Trainer:** Yes, that one is the women's locker room, and the other one is for men.
— **Customer:** Is there a water fountain?
— **Trainer:** Of course! We have two—one in the far-left corner and another near the entrance. Plus, there's a café downstairs.
— **Customer:** Are there classes on weekends too?

- **Trainer:** Yes, but Saturday classes are very popular, so I recommend booking in advance to secure a spot.
- **Customer:** Got it! I'll book a yoga class now.

▶ CONVERSATION 2

- **Trainer:** Is this your first time doing Pilates?
- **Student:** Yes, it's my first time.
- **Trainer:** Do you have any health issues?
- **Student:** No, nothing serious.
- **Trainer:** Any back problems?
- **Student:** Sometimes my back hurts a little because I sit for long hours working on my computer.
- **Trainer:** Understood. This class is for beginners. Today, we'll focus on stretching the arms, legs, neck, and back muscles.
- **Student:** How long is the class?
- **Trainer:** It lasts 45 minutes.
- **Student:** Do I need to bring anything?
- **Trainer:** No, we provide all the necessary equipment in the studio.
- **Student:** Can I bring a water bottle?
- **Trainer:** Yes, of course.
- **Student:** Do I need to book in advance?
- **Trainer:** Yes, reservations are required. You can book at the front desk, on our website, or through the gym's app.

EXERCISES

1. Write the name of 5 things that you can normally find in a gym.

1. _____

2. _____

3. _____

4. _____

5. _____

2. Imagine you work in a gym and you have to advise the following people:

- I want to lose weight quickly.

_____

_____

- I would like to have more flexibility.

_____

_____

- I like intense classes.

_____

_____

- My intention is to have bigger muscles.

  _____

  _____

- I don't like group classes but I need motivation and a person by my side.

  _____

  _____

LANGUAGES

▶ CONVERSATION 1

— **Jane:** You're studying Italian now, right?

— **Sebastian:** Yes, I like learning languages, and Italian is easy for me.

— **Jane:** How many languages do you speak in total?

— **Sebastian:** Well, I speak Spanish, English, and Greek very well. Then I know some French, and now I'm studying Italian.

— **Jane:** You speak Greek too?

— **Sebastian:** Yes, because my grandparents are Greek.

— **Jane:** And don't you mix up the languages when you speak?

— **Sebastian:** Sometimes with Spanish and Italian, but usually not.

— **Jane:** Yeah, they're a bit similar.

— **Sebastian:** What about you, Jane?

— **Jane:** I speak English because I'm Australian, but as you know, I'm studying Spanish here in Mallorca.

— **Sebastian:** You speak very well.

— **Jane:** Thanks! My teacher is really good, and I love learning new things.

— **Sebastian:** Do you take Spanish classes every day?

— **Jane:** Yes, it's a Spanish school in the city center.

— **Sebastian:** And how many students are in your class?

— **Jane:** It's not a big group. There are six of us, and everyone speaks well, but I'm very competitive and want to be the best.

— **Sebastian:** That's a great motivation.

▶ CONVERSATION 2

— **Teacher:** Where did you study English?
— **Student:** At school. Then at university for two years.
— **Teacher:** And do you like it?
— **Student:** I love it. In general, I really enjoy learning languages.
— **Teacher:** Why?
— **Student:** Because it's very practical. I can understand books, movies, and have conversations with people from other countries.
— **Teacher:** What's the hardest part of English for you?
— **Student:** I think almost all students struggle to remember the use of prepositions.
— **Teacher:** And how do you memorize the vocabulary?
— **Student:** I use a very old-fashioned method: pen and paper. Writing down the words and repeating them constantly works best for me.
— **Teacher:** Do you have any other effective methods?
— **Student:** Everyone has their own way of learning, but for me, listening to songs in the language I'm studying is a really fun way to learn.

EXERCISES

1. Please answer the following questions.

- Have you studied languages at school?

- Why do you study English?

- What activities are most useful for you?

- What do you think is the most difficult thing about English?

- Do you think there are easy and difficult languages to learn? Which ones?

- What do you recommend to a student who has never studied English?

2. Write a short paragraph comparing your native language with English (grammar, vocabulary, sounds, etc.)

_____

_____

_____

_____

_____

_____

_____

_____

THIS WEEK

▶ CONVERSATION 1

— **Daniel:** Today is Friday, right?

— **Mark:** Yes, it's incredible how fast the days go by.

— **Daniel:** How has your week been?

— **Mark:** Really good, actually. I got a lot done at the office with my colleagues. For example, we had a meeting with the CEO, and he told us that this year's results are very positive.

— **Daniel:** Did you travel to Seattle for the meeting with the CEO?

— **Mark:** No, he came to Denver to talk to us.

— **Daniel:** Lucky you.

— **Mark:** Yeah, we've been traveling too much in the past few weeks, and now we're a bit tired. What about you? Did you have a good week?

— **Daniel:** Work was pretty calm, but I did a lot of sports, so I'm also a little tired.

— **Mark:** Have you been running every day?

— **Daniel:** Yes, my wife and I have gone running every day for 45 minutes.

— **Mark:** Have you been training for next week's race?

— **Daniel:** Yes, I promised my wife I'd run with her.

— **Mark:** You're lucky. I haven't done any sports this week because I haven't had time, but next week will be different.

▶ CONVERSATION 2

— **Emma:** Have you done all the school exercises this week?

— **Jake:** Yes, I finished them this morning.

— **Emma:** I haven't done anything yet.

— **Jake:** Nothing at all?

— **Emma:** Well, I completed the first exercise, but nothing else.

— **Jake:** And what have you been doing for the rest of the week?

— **Emma:** I watched a really good TV series.

— **Jake:** You didn't do the exercises because you were watching TV?

— **Emma:** No, I also helped my mom around the house and took care of my little brother.

— **Jake:** I see, but you still had plenty of time to finish your homework.

— **Emma:** That's true. Now I need your help, Jake.

— **Jake:** My help?

— **Emma:** Yes, now that you're done, you can help me with the exercises.

— **Jake:** Are you serious?

— **Emma:** I've always helped you, Jake.

— **Jake:** Fiiine, alright.

1. **Complete the sentences with the correct form of the Present Perfect (e.g. "I have eaten").**

1. I _____ never _____ to Miami. People say that it is a very beautiful city.

2. This morning _____ the news on television.

3. _____ the exercises for English class? They're very difficult, aren't they?

4. The director _____ that tomorrow we can work from home.

5. I _____ foreign languages.

2. Write at least 5 things you have done today. Use the Past Perfect (e.g. "I have spoken").

YESTERDAY

▶ CONVERSATION 1

- **Brian:** I went to bed at 2 AM yesterday.
- **Ethan:** Why so late?
- **Brian:** I was working all night until I finished the job.
- **Ethan:** Did you work during the day too?
- **Brian:** No, that was the problem. I had to go to my son's school, so I couldn't work during the day.
- **Ethan:** I get it. We had to go two months ago, and I couldn't get much work done that day either.
- **Brian:** Yeah, I got home pretty late yesterday, made dinner for my wife and son, watched the news on TV, and then started working at 10 PM.
- **Ethan:** Must have been something important.
- **Brian:** Yes, I had to prepare a report for this morning's meeting.
- **Ethan:** Did you finish it on time?
- **Brian:** Yes, luckily I did, and the meeting went pretty well.

▶ CONVERSATION 2

— **Hannah:** Last night's concert was amazing!
— **Rachel:** Did you go alone?
— **Hannah:** No, I went with my sister and her boyfriend.
— **Rachel:** Was it a long concert?
— **Hannah:** It lasted about two hours.
— **Rachel:** He's a great singer. I went to one of his concerts two years ago, and I loved it.
— **Hannah:** Yeah, and last night, he had some amazing musicians with him. They played all the songs from the new album. They were all fantastic.
— **Rachel:** Did your sister like the concert too?
— **Hannah:** She loved it! It was her idea to go, and she was the one who bought the tickets.
— **Rachel:** What about her boyfriend?
— **Hannah:** Well, I don't think he enjoyed it that much, but he went because my sister is a huge fan.
— **Rachel:** My boyfriend was the same. I think he's one of those artists who's more popular with girls than with guys.
— **Hannah:** Yeah, I think so too. But my sister's boyfriend was really sweet about it and didn't complain at all.

EXERCISES

1. Complete the sentences with the correct form of the Simple Past (e.g. "I spoke").

1. Last night I _____ a very good Argentine film.

2. Last year I _____ on vacation to Florida.

3. I _____ the food in this restaurant.

4. Yesterday I _____ a lot of exercise and today my back hurts.

5. We _____ this house 3 years ago.

2. Write what you did yesterday. Use the Preterite Indefinite (e.g. "I worked").

_____

_____

_____

_____

_____

_____

_____

_____

_____

BEFORE & AFTER

▶ CONVERSATION 1

- **Natalie:** Do you remember your first mobile phone?
- **Claire:** Yes, it was huge.
- **Natalie:** And it was really heavy, right?
- **Claire:** It didn't have many features; you could only make calls and send text messages.
- **Natalie:** Do you remember what color it was?
- **Claire:** If I remember correctly, mine was green, but I'm not sure.
- **Natalie:** Mine was blue with white buttons.
- **Claire:** I remember the screen wasn't in color; it was just black and white.
- **Natalie:** And they were so expensive back then, do you remember?
- **Claire:** Yeah, though now there are still some really expensive phones. You can also get decent ones for very little money.
- **Natalie:** I loved my phone and the ringtones it had.
- **Claire:** They were so simple compared to today's phones…
- **Natalie:** Yeah, I agree. Now phones have so many complicated features. Just taking a simple picture has so many options that it's confusing.
- **Claire:** Well, we sound like two old ladies talking about the past.
- **Natalie:** Haha, you're absolutely right!

▶ CONVERSATION 2

— **Leila:** This city has changed so much…

— **Vivian:** Yeah, a lot. There didn't use to be so much traffic, and now there are traffic jams downtown and at the city exits every day.

— **Leila:** And public transport wasn't so crowded either. Now we're packed in like sardines.

— **Vivian:** The good thing is that now we have more parks and green spaces because before, we had to play in the plazas.

— **Leila:** Yeah, my siblings and I used to play ball in the street, and when a car came by, we would just move aside.

— **Vivian:** That was a bit dangerous, don't you think?

— **Leila:** Well, not really. Today, I think it's more dangerous to go out at night, for example.

— **Vivian:** My parents never let me go out at night. Only when I turned 18 could I stay out until midnight.

— **Leila:** What I loved the most was the city festival when my whole family would come over, and I got to play with my cousins. My parents' house was completely full, and every bed had two people sleeping in it.

— **Vivian:** I loved Christmas because we would go to my aunt's house, and all my cousins were there. We had so much fun playing and watching TV together.

— **Leila:** Such wonderful memories!

1. Answer the following questions

- What was your first house like?

  _____

- Who was your idol when you were little?

  _____

- What was your first mobile phone like?

  _____

- What was your first computer like?

  _____

- Who was your best friend when you were little?

  _____

- What did you like to play when you were 12?

  _____

2. Think about what life was like before there was internet in homes and write a paragraph about it.

_____

_____

_____

_____

_____

_____

_____

_____

_____

www.ingramcontent.com/pod-product-compliance
Lightning Source LLC
Chambersburg PA
CBHW071227090426
42736CB00014B/3004